D0935063

Give Thanks to the Lord

A Five-Minute
Daily Gratitude Journal

Good Books

New York, New York

Copyright © 2019 by Good Books

All rights reserved. No part of this book may be reproduced in any manner without the express written consent of the publisher, except in the case of brief excerpts in critical reviews or articles. All inquiries should be addressed to Good Books, 307 West 36th Street, 11th Floor, New York, NY 10018.

Good Books books may be purchased in bulk at special discounts for sales promotion, corporate gifts, fund-raising, or educational purposes. Special editions can also be created to specifications. For details, contact the Special Sales Department, Good Books, 307 West 36th Street, 11th Floor, New York, NY 10018 or info@skyhorsepublishing.com.

Good Books is an imprint of Skyhorse Publishing, Inc.®, a Delaware corporation.

Visit our website at www.goodbooks.com.

10 9 8 7 6 5 4 3 2 1

Library of Congress Cataloging-in-Publication Data is available on file.

Print ISBN: 978-1-68099-481-0

Cover design by Abigail Gehring
Cover image courtesy of Getty Images

Printed in China

Scriptures are taken from the KING JAMES VERSION (KJV): KING JAMES VERSION, public domain.

Give Thanks Daily

Have you ever noticed how much better your day goes when you start off with giving thanks? There is something about taking just a few minutes to thank God for all He has done—and is doing—that changes your perspective on everything. Intentional thanksgiving is a discipline, something you have to remind yourself to do, to practice daily. This book can help.

On every spread you'll find a Bible verse to meditate on; you may even wish to spend the week committing it to memory. Below that are a few lines for every day of the week. Jot down the date and then write what you are grateful for. If you need more space on some days, use the extra journal pages at the end of the book. Not only will your heart be refreshed and strengthened as you give God the glory He deserves, but you'll have a reminder of God's goodness to look back on later when the going gets tough.

O give thanks unto the Lord; for he is good:
because his mercy endureth for ever.

PSALM 118:1

I AM GRATEFUL FOR . . .   DATE: _____

_____

_____

_____

I AM GRATEFUL FOR . . .   DATE: _____

_____

_____

_____

I AM GRATEFUL FOR . . .   DATE: _____

_____

_____

_____

I AM GRATEFUL FOR . . .   DATE: _____

_____

_____

_____

I AM GRATEFUL FOR . . .   DATE: _____

_____

_____

_____

I AM GRATEFUL FOR . . .   DATE: _____

_____

_____

_____

I AM GRATEFUL FOR . . .   DATE: _____

_____

_____

_____

. . . his compassions fail not. They are new every morning: great is thy faithfulness.
—LAMENTATIONS 3:22–23

I AM GRATEFUL FOR . . .   DATE: _____

_____
_____
_____

I AM GRATEFUL FOR . . .   DATE: _____

_____
_____
_____

I AM GRATEFUL FOR . . .   DATE: _____

_____
_____
_____

I AM GRATEFUL FOR . . .　　　　　　　　DATE: _____

_____
_____
_____

I AM GRATEFUL FOR . . .　　　　　　　　DATE: _____

_____
_____
_____

I AM GRATEFUL FOR . . .　　　　　　　　DATE: _____

_____
_____
_____

I AM GRATEFUL FOR . . .　　　　　　　　DATE: _____

_____
_____
_____

. . . in every thing by prayer and supplication with thanksgiving let your requests be made known unto God.

—Philippians 4:6

I AM GRATEFUL FOR . . .   DATE: _____

_____
_____
_____

I AM GRATEFUL FOR . . .   DATE: _____

_____
_____
_____

I AM GRATEFUL FOR . . .   DATE: _____

_____
_____
_____

I AM GRATEFUL FOR . . .   DATE: _____

_____
_____
_____

I AM GRATEFUL FOR . . .   DATE: _____

_____
_____
_____

I AM GRATEFUL FOR . . .   DATE: _____

_____
_____
_____

I AM GRATEFUL FOR . . .   DATE: _____

_____
_____
_____

For thou, Lord, hast made me glad through thy work: I will triumph in the works of thy hands.
—PSALM 92:4

I AM GRATEFUL FOR . . .   DATE: _____

_____

_____

_____

I AM GRATEFUL FOR . . .   DATE: _____

_____

_____

_____

I AM GRATEFUL FOR . . .   DATE: _____

_____

_____

_____

I AM GRATEFUL FOR . . .　　　　　　　　　　　DATE: _____

_____
_____
_____

I AM GRATEFUL FOR . . .　　　　　　　　　　　DATE: _____

_____
_____
_____

I AM GRATEFUL FOR . . .　　　　　　　　　　　DATE: _____

_____
_____
_____

I AM GRATEFUL FOR . . .　　　　　　　　　　　DATE: _____

_____
_____
_____

And he hath put a new song in my mouth . . .
—Psalm 40:3

I AM GRATEFUL FOR . . .   DATE: _____

_____

_____

_____

I AM GRATEFUL FOR . . .   DATE: _____

_____

_____

_____

I AM GRATEFUL FOR . . .   DATE: _____

_____

_____

_____

I AM GRATEFUL FOR . . .   DATE: _____

_____

_____

_____

I AM GRATEFUL FOR . . .   DATE: _____

_____

_____

_____

I AM GRATEFUL FOR . . .   DATE: _____

_____

_____

_____

I AM GRATEFUL FOR . . .   DATE: _____

_____

_____

_____

Now the Lord is that Spirit: and where the Spirit
of the Lord is, there is liberty.
—2 Corinthians 3:17

I AM GRATEFUL FOR . . .   DATE: _____

_____

_____

_____

I AM GRATEFUL FOR . . .   DATE: _____

_____

_____

_____

I AM GRATEFUL FOR . . .   DATE: _____

_____

_____

_____

I AM GRATEFUL FOR . . .   DATE: _____

_____

_____

_____

I AM GRATEFUL FOR . . .   DATE: _____

_____

_____

_____

I AM GRATEFUL FOR . . .   DATE: _____

_____

_____

_____

I AM GRATEFUL FOR . . .   DATE: _____

_____

_____

_____

When thou passest through the waters,
I will be with thee; and through the rivers,
they shall not overflow thee . . .
—ISAIAH 43:2

I AM GRATEFUL FOR . . .   DATE: _____

_____

_____

_____

I AM GRATEFUL FOR . . .   DATE: _____

_____

_____

_____

I AM GRATEFUL FOR . . .   DATE: _____

_____

_____

_____

I AM GRATEFUL FOR . . .   DATE: _____

_____
_____
_____

I AM GRATEFUL FOR . . .   DATE: _____

_____
_____
_____

I AM GRATEFUL FOR . . .   DATE: _____

_____
_____
_____

I AM GRATEFUL FOR . . .   DATE: _____

_____
_____
_____

While I live will I praise the Lord: I will sing praises unto my God while I have any being.
—PSALM 146:2

I AM GRATEFUL FOR . . .   DATE: _____

_____
_____
_____

I AM GRATEFUL FOR . . .   DATE: _____

_____
_____
_____

I AM GRATEFUL FOR . . .   DATE: _____

_____
_____
_____

I AM GRATEFUL FOR . . .   DATE: _____

_____
_____
_____

I AM GRATEFUL FOR . . .   DATE: _____

_____
_____
_____

I AM GRATEFUL FOR . . .   DATE: _____

_____
_____
_____

I AM GRATEFUL FOR . . .   DATE: _____

_____
_____
_____

Be of good courage, and he shall strengthen your heart, all ye that hope in the Lord.

—Psalm 31:24

I AM GRATEFUL FOR . . .   DATE: _____

_____

_____

_____

I AM GRATEFUL FOR . . .   DATE: _____

_____

_____

_____

I AM GRATEFUL FOR . . .   DATE: _____

_____

_____

_____

I AM GRATEFUL FOR . . .   DATE: _____

_____
_____
_____

I AM GRATEFUL FOR . . .   DATE: _____

_____
_____
_____

I AM GRATEFUL FOR . . .   DATE: _____

_____
_____
_____

I AM GRATEFUL FOR . . .   DATE: _____

_____
_____
_____

Let the saints be joyful in glory:
let them sing aloud upon their beds.
PSALM 149:5

I AM GRATEFUL FOR . . .   DATE: _____

_____

_____

_____

I AM GRATEFUL FOR . . .   DATE: _____

_____

_____

_____

I AM GRATEFUL FOR . . .   DATE: _____

_____

_____

_____

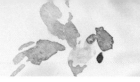

I AM GRATEFUL FOR . . .   DATE: _____

_____
_____
_____

I AM GRATEFUL FOR . . .   DATE: _____

_____
_____
_____

I AM GRATEFUL FOR . . .   DATE: _____

_____
_____
_____

I AM GRATEFUL FOR . . .   DATE: _____

_____
_____
_____

In all thy ways acknowledge him,
and he shall direct thy paths.

PROVERBS 3:6

I AM GRATEFUL FOR . . .   DATE: _____

_____

_____

_____

I AM GRATEFUL FOR . . .   DATE: _____

_____

_____

_____

I AM GRATEFUL FOR . . .   DATE: _____

_____

_____

_____

I AM GRATEFUL FOR . . .   DATE: _____

_____

_____

_____

I AM GRATEFUL FOR . . .   DATE: _____

_____

_____

_____

I AM GRATEFUL FOR . . .   DATE: _____

_____

_____

_____

I AM GRATEFUL FOR . . .   DATE: _____

_____

_____

_____

Come unto me, all ye that labour and are heavy laden, and I will give you rest.

Matthew 11:28

I AM GRATEFUL FOR . . .   DATE: _____

_____
_____
_____

I AM GRATEFUL FOR . . .   DATE: _____

_____
_____
_____

I AM GRATEFUL FOR . . .   DATE: _____

_____
_____
_____

I AM GRATEFUL FOR . . .   DATE: _____

_____
_____
_____

I AM GRATEFUL FOR . . .   DATE: _____

_____
_____
_____

I AM GRATEFUL FOR . . .   DATE: _____

_____
_____
_____

I AM GRATEFUL FOR . . .   DATE: _____

_____
_____
_____

Peace I leave with you, my peace I give unto you: not as the world giveth, give I unto you. Let not your heart be troubled, neither let it be afraid.

JOHN 14:27

I AM GRATEFUL FOR . . .   DATE: _____

_____
_____
_____

I AM GRATEFUL FOR . . .   DATE: _____

_____
_____
_____

I AM GRATEFUL FOR . . .   DATE: _____

_____
_____
_____

I AM GRATEFUL FOR . . .   DATE: _____

_____

_____

_____

I AM GRATEFUL FOR . . .   DATE: _____

_____

_____

_____

I AM GRATEFUL FOR . . .   DATE: _____

_____

_____

_____

I AM GRATEFUL FOR . . .   DATE: _____

_____

_____

_____

Restore unto me the joy of thy salvation;
and uphold me with thy free spirit.

PSALM 51:12

I AM GRATEFUL FOR . . .   DATE: _____

_____

_____

_____

I AM GRATEFUL FOR . . .   DATE: _____

_____

_____

_____

I AM GRATEFUL FOR . . .   DATE: _____

_____

_____

_____

I AM GRATEFUL FOR . . .   DATE: _____

_____

_____

_____

I AM GRATEFUL FOR . . .   DATE: _____

_____

_____

_____

I AM GRATEFUL FOR . . .   DATE: _____

_____

_____

_____

I AM GRATEFUL FOR . . .   DATE: _____

_____

_____

_____

Be still, and know that I am God: I will be exalted among the heathen, I will be exalted in the earth.

PSALM 46:10

I AM GRATEFUL FOR . . .   DATE: _____

_____

_____

_____

I AM GRATEFUL FOR . . .   DATE: _____

_____

_____

_____

I AM GRATEFUL FOR . . .   DATE: _____

_____

_____

_____

I AM GRATEFUL FOR . . .   DATE: _____

_____

_____

_____

I AM GRATEFUL FOR . . .   DATE: _____

_____

_____

_____

I AM GRATEFUL FOR . . .   DATE: _____

_____

_____

_____

I AM GRATEFUL FOR . . .   DATE: _____

_____

_____

_____

God is our refuge and strength,
a very present help in trouble.
PSALM 46:1

I AM GRATEFUL FOR . . .   DATE: _____

_____
_____
_____

I AM GRATEFUL FOR . . .   DATE: _____

_____
_____
_____

I AM GRATEFUL FOR . . .   DATE: _____

_____
_____
_____

I AM GRATEFUL FOR . . .   DATE: _____

_____

_____

_____

I AM GRATEFUL FOR . . .   DATE: _____

_____

_____

_____

I AM GRATEFUL FOR . . .   DATE: _____

_____

_____

_____

I AM GRATEFUL FOR . . .   DATE: _____

_____

_____

_____

For God hath not given us the spirit of fear; but of power, and of love, and of a sound mind.

2 Timothy 1:7

I AM GRATEFUL FOR . . .   DATE: _____

_____

_____

_____

I AM GRATEFUL FOR . . .   DATE: _____

_____

_____

_____

I AM GRATEFUL FOR . . .   DATE: _____

_____

_____

_____

I AM GRATEFUL FOR . . .   DATE: _____

_____
_____
_____

I AM GRATEFUL FOR . . .   DATE: _____

_____
_____
_____

I AM GRATEFUL FOR . . .   DATE: _____

_____
_____
_____

I AM GRATEFUL FOR . . .   DATE: _____

_____
_____
_____

My soul shall be satisfied as with marrow and fatness;
and my mouth shall praise thee with joyful lips:
PSALM 63:5

I AM GRATEFUL FOR . . .   DATE: _____

_____

_____

_____

I AM GRATEFUL FOR . . .   DATE: _____

_____

_____

_____

I AM GRATEFUL FOR . . .   DATE: _____

_____

_____

_____

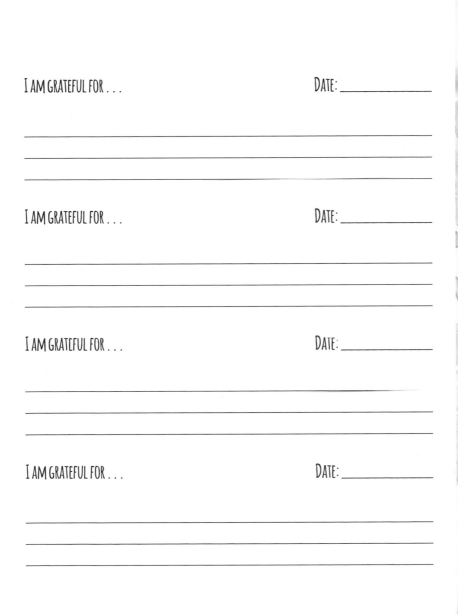

I AM GRATEFUL FOR . . .   DATE: _____

_____
_____
_____

I AM GRATEFUL FOR . . .   DATE: _____

_____
_____
_____

I AM GRATEFUL FOR . . .   DATE: _____

_____
_____
_____

I AM GRATEFUL FOR . . .   DATE: _____

_____
_____
_____

The Lord is on my side;
I will not fear: what can man do unto me?
PSALM 118:6

I AM GRATEFUL FOR . . .   DATE: _____

_____

_____

_____

I AM GRATEFUL FOR . . .   DATE: _____

_____

_____

_____

I AM GRATEFUL FOR . . .   DATE: _____

_____

_____

_____

I AM GRATEFUL FOR . . .   DATE: _____

_____
_____
_____

I AM GRATEFUL FOR . . .   DATE: _____

_____
_____
_____

I AM GRATEFUL FOR . . .   DATE: _____

_____
_____
_____

I AM GRATEFUL FOR . . .   DATE: _____

_____
_____
_____

O Lord, open thou my lips;
and my mouth shall shew forth thy praise.

PSALM 51:15

I AM GRATEFUL FOR . . .   DATE: _____

_____
_____
_____

I AM GRATEFUL FOR . . .   DATE: _____

_____
_____
_____

I AM GRATEFUL FOR . . .   DATE: _____

_____
_____
_____

I AM GRATEFUL FOR . . .   DATE: _____

_____
_____
_____
_____

I AM GRATEFUL FOR . . .   DATE: _____

_____
_____
_____
_____

I AM GRATEFUL FOR . . .   DATE: _____

_____
_____
_____
_____

I AM GRATEFUL FOR . . .   DATE: _____

_____
_____
_____
_____

The Lord is my strength and song,
and is become my salvation.
PSALM 118:14

I AM GRATEFUL FOR . . .   DATE: _____

_____
_____
_____

I AM GRATEFUL FOR . . .   DATE: _____

_____
_____
_____

I AM GRATEFUL FOR . . .   DATE: _____

_____
_____
_____

I AM GRATEFUL FOR . . .   DATE: _____

_____
_____
_____

I AM GRATEFUL FOR . . .   DATE: _____

_____
_____
_____

I AM GRATEFUL FOR . . .   DATE: _____

_____
_____
_____

I AM GRATEFUL FOR . . .   DATE: _____

_____
_____
_____

I will praise thee: for thou hast heard me,
and art become my salvation.

PSALM 118:21

I AM GRATEFUL FOR . . .   DATE: _____

_____

_____

_____

I AM GRATEFUL FOR . . .   DATE: _____

_____

_____

_____

I AM GRATEFUL FOR . . .   DATE: _____

_____

_____

_____

I AM GRATEFUL FOR . . .   DATE: _____

_____
_____
_____

I AM GRATEFUL FOR . . .   DATE: _____

_____
_____
_____

I AM GRATEFUL FOR . . .   DATE: _____

_____
_____
_____

I AM GRATEFUL FOR . . .   DATE: _____

_____
_____
_____

*Therefore my heart is glad, and my glory rejoiceth:
my flesh also shall rest in hope.*

PSALM 16:9

I AM GRATEFUL FOR . . .   DATE: _____

_____
_____
_____

I AM GRATEFUL FOR . . .   DATE: _____

_____
_____
_____

I AM GRATEFUL FOR . . .   DATE: _____

_____
_____
_____

I AM GRATEFUL FOR . . .   DATE: _____

_____

_____

_____

I AM GRATEFUL FOR . . .   DATE: _____

_____

_____

_____

I AM GRATEFUL FOR . . .   DATE: _____

_____

_____

_____

I AM GRATEFUL FOR . . .   DATE: _____

_____

_____

_____

This is the day which the Lord hath made;
we will rejoice and be glad in it.

PSALM 118:24

I AM GRATEFUL FOR . . .   DATE: _____

_____

_____

_____

I AM GRATEFUL FOR . . .   DATE: _____

_____

_____

_____

I AM GRATEFUL FOR . . .   DATE: _____

_____

_____

_____

I AM GRATEFUL FOR . . .   DATE: _____

_____

_____

_____

I AM GRATEFUL FOR . . .   DATE: _____

_____

_____

_____

I AM GRATEFUL FOR . . .   DATE: _____

_____

_____

_____

I AM GRATEFUL FOR . . .   DATE: _____

_____

_____

_____

Blessing, and glory, and wisdom, and thanksgiving, and honour, and power, and might, be unto our God for ever and ever. Amen.

REVELATION 7:12

I AM GRATEFUL FOR . . .   DATE: _____

_____

_____

_____

I AM GRATEFUL FOR . . .   DATE: _____

_____

_____

_____

I AM GRATEFUL FOR . . .   DATE: _____

_____

_____

_____

I AM GRATEFUL FOR . . .   DATE: _____

_____
_____
_____

I AM GRATEFUL FOR . . .   DATE: _____

_____
_____
_____

I AM GRATEFUL FOR . . .   DATE: _____

_____
_____
_____

I AM GRATEFUL FOR . . .   DATE: _____

_____
_____
_____

Thou art my God, and I will praise thee:
thou art my God, I will exalt thee.
PSALM 118:28

I AM GRATEFUL FOR . . .   DATE: _____

_____

_____

_____

I AM GRATEFUL FOR . . .   DATE: _____

_____

_____

_____

I AM GRATEFUL FOR . . .   DATE: _____

_____

_____

_____

I AM GRATEFUL FOR . . .   DATE: _____

_____

_____

_____

I AM GRATEFUL FOR . . .   DATE: _____

_____

_____

_____

I AM GRATEFUL FOR . . .   DATE: _____

_____

_____

_____

I AM GRATEFUL FOR . . .   DATE: _____

_____

_____

_____

. . . for with the Lord there is mercy,
and with him is plenteous redemption.
PSALM 130:7

I AM GRATEFUL FOR . . .   DATE: _____

_____

_____

_____

I AM GRATEFUL FOR . . .   DATE: _____

_____

_____

_____

I AM GRATEFUL FOR . . .   DATE: _____

_____

_____

_____

I AM GRATEFUL FOR . . .   DATE: _____

_____
_____
_____

I AM GRATEFUL FOR . . .   DATE: _____

_____
_____
_____

I AM GRATEFUL FOR . . .   DATE: _____

_____
_____
_____

I AM GRATEFUL FOR . . .   DATE: _____

_____
_____
_____

I will praise thee; for I am fearfully and wonderfully made: marvellous are thy works; and that my soul knoweth right well.

PSALM 139:14

I AM GRATEFUL FOR . . .   DATE: _____

_____

_____

_____

I AM GRATEFUL FOR . . .   DATE: _____

_____

_____

_____

I AM GRATEFUL FOR . . .   DATE: _____

_____

_____

_____

I AM GRATEFUL FOR . . .   DATE: _____

_____

_____

_____

I AM GRATEFUL FOR . . .   DATE: _____

_____

_____

_____

I AM GRATEFUL FOR . . .   DATE: _____

_____

_____

_____

I AM GRATEFUL FOR . . .   DATE: _____

_____

_____

_____

And we know that all things work together for good to them that love God, to them who are the called according to his purpose.

ROMANS 8:28

I AM GRATEFUL FOR . . .   DATE: _____

_____

_____

_____

I AM GRATEFUL FOR . . .   DATE: _____

_____

_____

_____

I AM GRATEFUL FOR . . .   DATE: _____

_____

_____

_____

I AM GRATEFUL FOR . . .   DATE: _____

_____
_____
_____

I AM GRATEFUL FOR . . .   DATE: _____

_____
_____
_____

I AM GRATEFUL FOR . . .   DATE: _____

_____
_____
_____

I AM GRATEFUL FOR . . .   DATE: _____

_____
_____
_____

Mercy and truth are met together; righteousness and peace have kissed each other.

PSALM 85:10

I AM GRATEFUL FOR . . .   DATE: _____

_____

_____

_____

I AM GRATEFUL FOR . . .   DATE: _____

_____

_____

_____

I AM GRATEFUL FOR . . .   DATE: _____

_____

_____

_____

I AM GRATEFUL FOR . . .   DATE: _____

_____

_____

_____

I AM GRATEFUL FOR . . .   DATE: _____

_____

_____

_____

I AM GRATEFUL FOR . . .   DATE: _____

_____

_____

_____

I AM GRATEFUL FOR . . .   DATE: _____

_____

_____

_____

For he that is mighty hath done to me great things; and holy is his name. And his mercy is on them that fear him from generation to generation.

LUKE 1:49–50

I AM GRATEFUL FOR . . .   DATE: _____

_____

_____

_____

I AM GRATEFUL FOR . . .   DATE: _____

_____

_____

_____

I AM GRATEFUL FOR . . .   DATE: _____

_____

_____

_____

I AM GRATEFUL FOR . . .   DATE: _____

_____

_____

_____

I AM GRATEFUL FOR . . .   DATE: _____

_____

_____

_____

I AM GRATEFUL FOR . . .   DATE: _____

_____

_____

_____

I AM GRATEFUL FOR . . .   DATE: _____

_____

_____

_____

Thou wilt shew me the path of life: in thy presence is fulness of joy; at thy right hand there are pleasures for evermore.

PSALM 16:11

I AM GRATEFUL FOR . . .   DATE: _____

_____

_____

_____

I AM GRATEFUL FOR . . .   DATE: _____

_____

_____

_____

I AM GRATEFUL FOR . . .   DATE: _____

_____

_____

_____

I AM GRATEFUL FOR . . .   DATE: _____

_____
_____
_____

I AM GRATEFUL FOR . . .   DATE: _____

_____
_____
_____

I AM GRATEFUL FOR . . .   DATE: _____

_____
_____
_____

I AM GRATEFUL FOR . . .   DATE: _____

_____
_____
_____

I can do all things through Christ which strengtheneth me.

PHILIPPIANS 4:13

I AM GRATEFUL FOR . . .   DATE: _____

_____

_____

_____

I AM GRATEFUL FOR . . .   DATE: _____

_____

_____

_____

I AM GRATEFUL FOR . . .   DATE: _____

_____

_____

_____

I AM GRATEFUL FOR . . .   DATE: _____

_____
_____
_____

I AM GRATEFUL FOR . . .   DATE: _____

_____
_____
_____

I AM GRATEFUL FOR . . .   DATE: _____

_____
_____
_____

I AM GRATEFUL FOR . . .   DATE: _____

_____
_____
_____

Fear not: for I have redeemed thee,
I have called thee by thy name; thou art mine.
ISAIAH 43:1

I AM GRATEFUL FOR . . .   DATE: _____

_____

_____

_____

I AM GRATEFUL FOR . . .   DATE: _____

_____

_____

_____

I AM GRATEFUL FOR . . .   DATE: _____

_____

_____

_____

I AM GRATEFUL FOR . . .   DATE: _____

_____
_____
_____

I AM GRATEFUL FOR . . .   DATE: _____

_____
_____
_____

I AM GRATEFUL FOR . . .   DATE: _____

_____
_____
_____

I AM GRATEFUL FOR . . .   DATE: _____

_____
_____
_____

I will both lay me down in peace, and sleep: for thou, Lord, only makest me dwell in safety.

PSALM 4:8

I AM GRATEFUL FOR . . .   DATE: _____

_____

_____

_____

I AM GRATEFUL FOR . . .   DATE: _____

_____

_____

_____

I AM GRATEFUL FOR . . .   DATE: _____

_____

_____

_____

I AM GRATEFUL FOR . . .   DATE: _____

_____

_____

_____

I AM GRATEFUL FOR . . .   DATE: _____

_____

_____

_____

I AM GRATEFUL FOR . . .   DATE: _____

_____

_____

_____

I AM GRATEFUL FOR . . .   DATE: _____

_____

_____

_____

Rest in the Lord, and wait patiently for him . . .
PSALM 37:7

I AM GRATEFUL FOR . . .   DATE: _____

_____
_____
_____

I AM GRATEFUL FOR . . .   DATE: _____

_____
_____
_____

I AM GRATEFUL FOR . . .   DATE: _____

_____
_____
_____

I AM GRATEFUL FOR . . .   Date: _____

_____
_____
_____

I AM GRATEFUL FOR . . .   Date: _____

_____
_____
_____

I AM GRATEFUL FOR . . .   Date: _____

_____
_____
_____

I AM GRATEFUL FOR . . .   Date: _____

_____
_____
_____

Return unto thy rest, O my soul; for the Lord hath dealt bountifully with thee.

PSALM 116:7

I AM GRATEFUL FOR . . .   DATE: _____

_____

_____

_____

I AM GRATEFUL FOR . . .   DATE: _____

_____

_____

_____

I AM GRATEFUL FOR . . .   DATE: _____

_____

_____

_____

I AM GRATEFUL FOR . . .   DATE: _____

_____
_____
_____

I AM GRATEFUL FOR . . .   DATE: _____

_____
_____
_____

I AM GRATEFUL FOR . . .   DATE: _____

_____
_____
_____

I AM GRATEFUL FOR . . .   DATE: _____

_____
_____
_____

But rather seek ye the kingdom of God;
and all these things shall be added unto you.
Luke 12:31

I AM GRATEFUL FOR . . .   DATE: _____

_____
_____
_____

I AM GRATEFUL FOR . . .   DATE: _____

_____
_____
_____

I AM GRATEFUL FOR . . .   DATE: _____

_____
_____
_____

I AM GRATEFUL FOR . . .   DATE: _____

_____
_____
_____

I AM GRATEFUL FOR . . .   DATE: _____

_____
_____
_____

I AM GRATEFUL FOR . . .   DATE: _____

_____
_____
_____

I AM GRATEFUL FOR . . .   DATE: _____

_____
_____
_____

There is therefore now no condemnation to them which are in Christ Jesus, who walk not after the flesh, but after the Spirit.

ROMANS 8:1

I AM GRATEFUL FOR . . .   DATE: _____

_____

_____

_____

I AM GRATEFUL FOR . . .   DATE: _____

_____

_____

_____

I AM GRATEFUL FOR . . .   DATE: _____

_____

_____

_____

I AM GRATEFUL FOR . . .   DATE: _____

_____
_____
_____

I AM GRATEFUL FOR . . .   DATE: _____

_____
_____
_____

I AM GRATEFUL FOR . . .   DATE: _____

_____
_____
_____

I AM GRATEFUL FOR . . .   DATE: _____

_____
_____
_____

. . . the joy of the Lord is your strength.
NEHEMIAH 8:10

I AM GRATEFUL FOR . . .   DATE: _____

_____

_____

_____

I AM GRATEFUL FOR . . .   DATE: _____

_____

_____

_____

I AM GRATEFUL FOR . . .   DATE: _____

_____

_____

_____

I AM GRATEFUL FOR . . .   DATE: _____

_____
_____
_____

I AM GRATEFUL FOR . . .   DATE: _____

_____
_____
_____

I AM GRATEFUL FOR . . .   DATE: _____

_____
_____
_____

I AM GRATEFUL FOR . . .   DATE: _____

_____
_____
_____

But my God shall supply all your need according to his riches in glory by Christ Jesus.

PHILIPPIANS 4:19

I AM GRATEFUL FOR . . .   DATE: _____

_____

_____

_____

I AM GRATEFUL FOR . . .   DATE: _____

_____

_____

_____

I AM GRATEFUL FOR . . .   DATE: _____

_____

_____

_____

I AM GRATEFUL FOR . . .   DATE: _____

_____
_____
_____

I AM GRATEFUL FOR . . .   DATE: _____

_____
_____
_____

I AM GRATEFUL FOR . . .   DATE: _____

_____
_____
_____

I AM GRATEFUL FOR . . .   DATE: _____

_____
_____
_____

He that spared not his own Son, but delivered him up for us all, how shall he not with him also freely give us all things?

ROMANS 8:32

I AM GRATEFUL FOR . . .   DATE: _____

_____

_____

_____

I AM GRATEFUL FOR . . .   DATE: _____

_____

_____

_____

I AM GRATEFUL FOR . . .   DATE: _____

_____

_____

_____

I AM GRATEFUL FOR . . .   DATE: _____

_____
_____
_____

I AM GRATEFUL FOR . . .   DATE: _____

_____
_____
_____

I AM GRATEFUL FOR . . .   DATE: _____

_____
_____
_____

I AM GRATEFUL FOR . . .   DATE: _____

_____
_____
_____

. . . your Father knoweth what things ye have need of, before ye ask him.

MATTHEW 6:8

I AM GRATEFUL FOR . . .   DATE: _____

_____

_____

_____

I AM GRATEFUL FOR . . .   DATE: _____

_____

_____

_____

I AM GRATEFUL FOR . . .   DATE: _____

_____

_____

_____

I AM GRATEFUL FOR . . .   DATE: _____

_____
_____
_____

I AM GRATEFUL FOR . . .   DATE: _____

_____
_____
_____

I AM GRATEFUL FOR . . .   DATE: _____

_____
_____
_____

I AM GRATEFUL FOR . . .   DATE: _____

_____
_____
_____

. . . for I have learned, in whatsoever state I am, therewith to be content.

PHILIPPIANS 4:11

I AM GRATEFUL FOR . . .   DATE: _____

_____

_____

_____

I AM GRATEFUL FOR . . .   DATE: _____

_____

_____

_____

I AM GRATEFUL FOR . . .   DATE: _____

_____

_____

_____

I AM GRATEFUL FOR . . .   Date: _____

_____
_____
_____

I AM GRATEFUL FOR . . .   Date: _____

_____
_____
_____

I AM GRATEFUL FOR . . .   Date: _____

_____
_____
_____

I AM GRATEFUL FOR . . .   Date: _____

_____
_____
_____

O Lord, how manifold are thy works! in wisdom hast thou made them all: the earth is full of thy riches.

PSALM 104:24

I AM GRATEFUL FOR . . .   DATE: _____

_____
_____
_____

I AM GRATEFUL FOR . . .   DATE: _____

_____
_____
_____

I AM GRATEFUL FOR . . .   DATE: _____

_____
_____
_____

I AM GRATEFUL FOR . . .   DATE: _____

_____
_____
_____

I AM GRATEFUL FOR . . .   DATE: _____

_____
_____
_____

I AM GRATEFUL FOR . . .   DATE: _____

_____
_____
_____

I AM GRATEFUL FOR . . .   DATE: _____

_____
_____
_____

I will praise thee, O Lord, with my whole heart; I will shew forth all thy marvellous works.

PSALM 9:1

I AM GRATEFUL FOR . . .   DATE: _____

_____

_____

_____

I AM GRATEFUL FOR . . .   DATE: _____

_____

_____

_____

I AM GRATEFUL FOR . . .   DATE: _____

_____

_____

_____

I AM GRATEFUL FOR . . .   DATE: _____

_____

_____

_____

I AM GRATEFUL FOR . . .   DATE: _____

_____

_____

_____

I AM GRATEFUL FOR . . .   DATE: _____

_____

_____

_____

I AM GRATEFUL FOR . . .   DATE: _____

_____

_____

_____

Let every thing that hath breath praise the Lord.
Praise ye the Lord.
PSALM 150:6

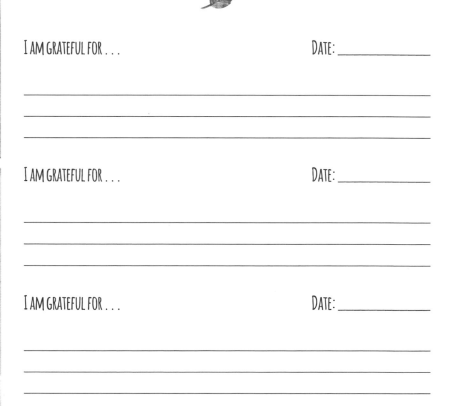

I AM GRATEFUL FOR . . .   DATE: _____

_____

_____

_____

I AM GRATEFUL FOR . . .   DATE: _____

_____

_____

_____

I AM GRATEFUL FOR . . .   DATE: _____

_____

_____

_____

I AM GRATEFUL FOR . . .   DATE: _____

_____

_____

_____

I AM GRATEFUL FOR . . .   DATE: _____

_____

_____

_____

I AM GRATEFUL FOR . . .   DATE: _____

_____

_____

_____

I AM GRATEFUL FOR . . .   DATE: _____

_____

_____

_____

Thou art worthy, O Lord, to receive glory and honour and power: for thou hast created all things, and for thy pleasure they are and were created.

REVELATIONS 4:11

I AM GRATEFUL FOR . . .   DATE: _____

_____
_____
_____

I AM GRATEFUL FOR . . .   DATE: _____

_____
_____
_____

I AM GRATEFUL FOR . . .   DATE: _____

_____
_____
_____

I AM GRATEFUL FOR . . .   DATE: _____

_____

_____

_____

I AM GRATEFUL FOR . . .   DATE: _____

_____

_____

_____

I AM GRATEFUL FOR . . .   DATE: _____

_____

_____

_____

I AM GRATEFUL FOR . . .   DATE: _____

_____

_____

_____

Every good gift and every perfect gift
is from above . . .

James 1:17

I AM GRATEFUL FOR . . .   DATE: _____

_____
_____
_____

I AM GRATEFUL FOR . . .   DATE: _____

_____
_____
_____

I AM GRATEFUL FOR . . .   DATE: _____

_____
_____
_____

I AM GRATEFUL FOR . . .   DATE: _____

_____

_____

_____

I AM GRATEFUL FOR . . .   DATE: _____

_____

_____

_____

I AM GRATEFUL FOR . . .   DATE: _____

_____

_____

_____

I AM GRATEFUL FOR . . .   DATE: _____

_____

_____

_____

Thou hast turned for me my mourning
into dancing . . .
PSALM 30:11

I AM GRATEFUL FOR . . .   DATE: _____

_____

_____

_____

I AM GRATEFUL FOR . . .   DATE: _____

_____

_____

_____

I AM GRATEFUL FOR . . .   DATE: _____

_____

_____

_____

I AM GRATEFUL FOR . . .   DATE: _____

_____
_____
_____

I AM GRATEFUL FOR . . .   DATE: _____

_____
_____
_____

I AM GRATEFUL FOR . . .   DATE: _____

_____
_____
_____

I AM GRATEFUL FOR . . .   DATE: _____

_____
_____
_____

Thou openest thine hand, and satisfiest
the desire of every living thing.
Psalm 145:16

I am grateful for . . .   Date: _____

_____
_____
_____

I am grateful for . . .   Date: _____

_____
_____
_____

I am grateful for . . .   Date: _____

_____
_____
_____

I AM GRATEFUL FOR . . .   DATE: _____

_____
_____
_____

I AM GRATEFUL FOR . . .   DATE: _____

_____
_____
_____

I AM GRATEFUL FOR . . .   DATE: _____

_____
_____
_____

I AM GRATEFUL FOR . . .   DATE: _____

_____
_____
_____

For he satisfieth the longing soul, and filleth the hungry soul with goodness.

PSALM 107:9

I AM GRATEFUL FOR . . .   DATE: _____

_____

_____

_____

I AM GRATEFUL FOR . . .   DATE: _____

_____

_____

_____

I AM GRATEFUL FOR . . .   DATE: _____

_____

_____

_____

I AM GRATEFUL FOR . . .   DATE: _____

_____
_____
_____

I AM GRATEFUL FOR . . .   DATE: _____

_____
_____
_____

I AM GRATEFUL FOR . . .   DATE: _____

_____
_____
_____

I AM GRATEFUL FOR . . .   DATE: _____

_____
_____
_____

Be careful for nothing; but in every thing by prayer and supplication with thanksgiving let your requests be made known unto God.

Philippians 4:6

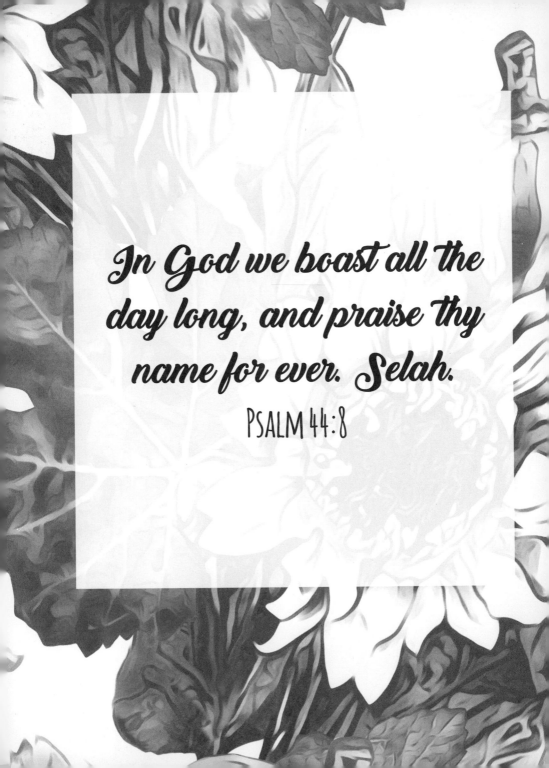

In God we boast all the day long, and praise thy name for ever. Selah.

PSALM 44:8

The heavens declare the glory of God; and the firmament sheweth his handywork.

PSALM 19:1

But I have trusted in thy mercy; my heart shall rejoice in thy salvation.

PSALM 13:5

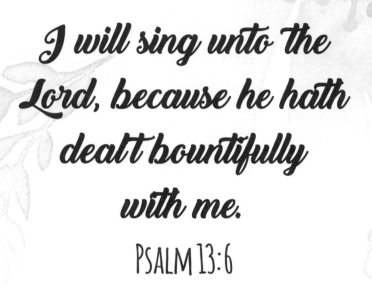

I will sing unto the Lord, because he hath dealt bountifully with me.

PSALM 13:6